AF270660

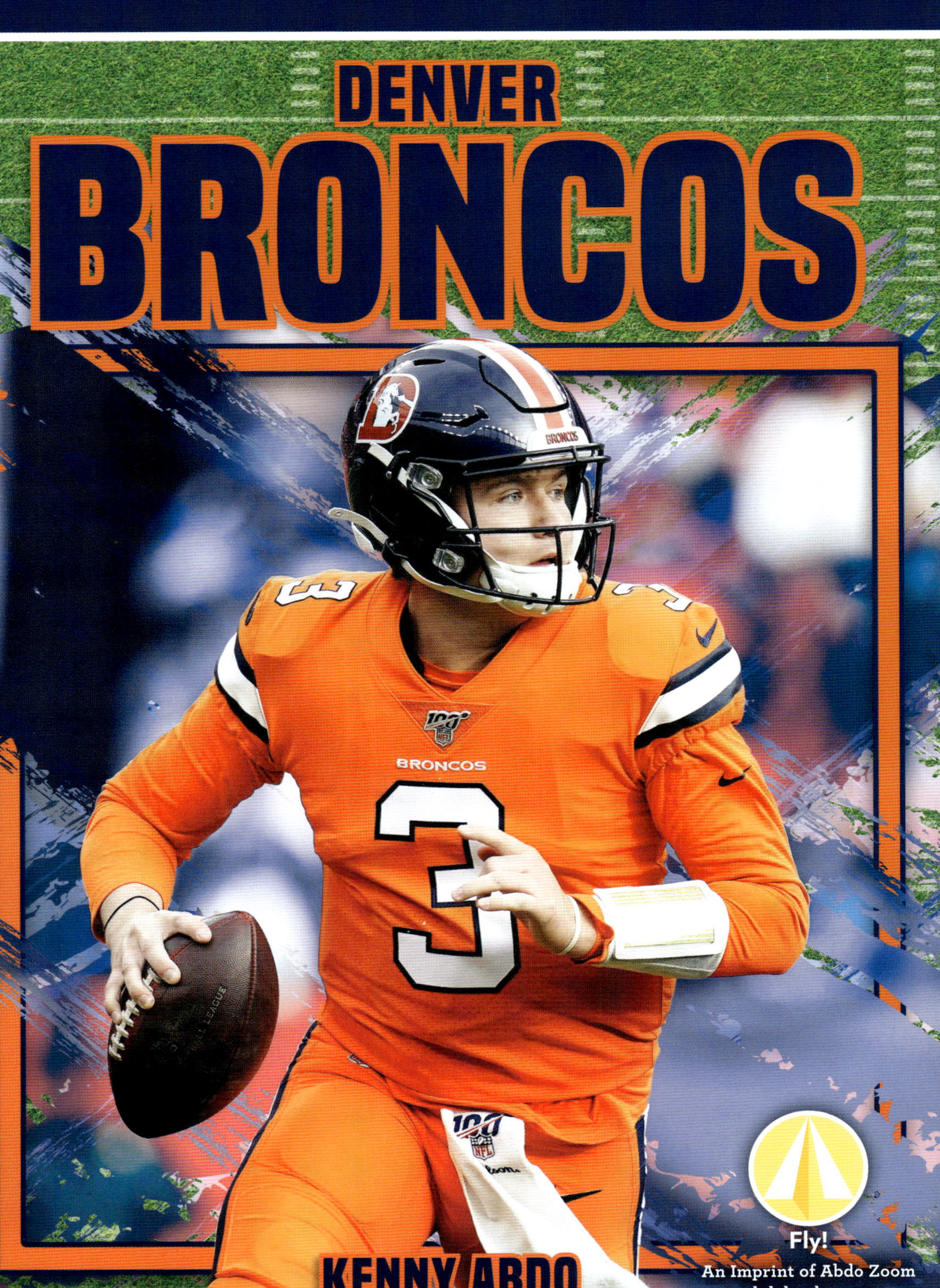

NFL TEAMS
DENVER BRONCOS
BRONCOS
KENNY ABDO
Fly!
An Imprint of Abdo Zoom
abdobooks.com

abdobooks.com

Published by Abdo Zoom, a division of ABDO, P.O. Box 398166, Minneapolis, Minnesota 55439. Copyright © 2022 by Abdo Consulting Group, Inc. International copyrights reserved in all countries. No part of this book may be reproduced in any form without written permission from the publisher. Fly!™ is a trademark and logo of Abdo Zoom.
Printed in China
052021
092021

THIS BOOK CONTAINS
RECYCLED MATERIALS

Photo Credits: iStock, Shutterstock PREMIER
Production Contributors: Kenny Abdo, Jennie Forsberg, Grace Hansen
Design Contributors: Candice Keimig, Neil Klinepier

Library of Congress Control Number: 2020919480

Publisher's Cataloging-in-Publication Data

Names: Abdo, Kenny, author.
Title: Denver Broncos / by Kenny Abdo
Description: Minneapolis, Minnesota : Abdo Zoom, 2022 | Series: NFL teams | Includes online resources and index.
Identifiers: ISBN 9781098224608 (lib. bdg.) | ISBN 9781098225544 (ebook) | ISBN 9781098226015 (Read-to-Me ebook)
Subjects: LCSH: Denver Broncos (Football team)--Juvenile literature. | National Football League--Juvenile literature. | Football teams--Juvenile literature. | American football--Juvenile literature. | Professional sports--Juvenile literature.
Classification: DDC 796.33264--dc23

TABLE OF CONTENTS

DENVER BRONCOS

Bucking off opponents and dashing down field, the Denver Broncos are a team that cannot be tamed.

With three **Super Bowl** wins under their belts, the Broncos are considered one of the best in the NFL.

NFL

KICK OFF

The Broncos were established in 1959 by businessman Bob Howsam. Howsam also owned the Denver Bears, a minor league baseball team.

The Broncos were one of the first teams in the American Football League (AFL). In 1970, the AFL merged with the NFL. The Broncos did not have a winning season until 1973.

The Broncos made it to the playoffs for the first time in 1977. They went on to their first **Super Bowl** that season but lost to the Dallas Cowboys 27–10.

TEAM RECAPS

Quarterback John Elway joined the Broncos in 1983. The team went to the **Super Bowl** three times in the 1980s but never won.

STUD
7
7

Eight years later, they got another chance at **Super Bowl** XXXII and won! The Broncos beat the Green Bay Packers 31–24. They won the next year's Super Bowl too, beating the Atlanta Falcons 34–19.

The Broncos scored 606 points during the 2013 season. That set an NFL record. They played and lost **Super Bowl** XLVIII to the Seahawks. But they won Super Bowl 50 against the Panthers!

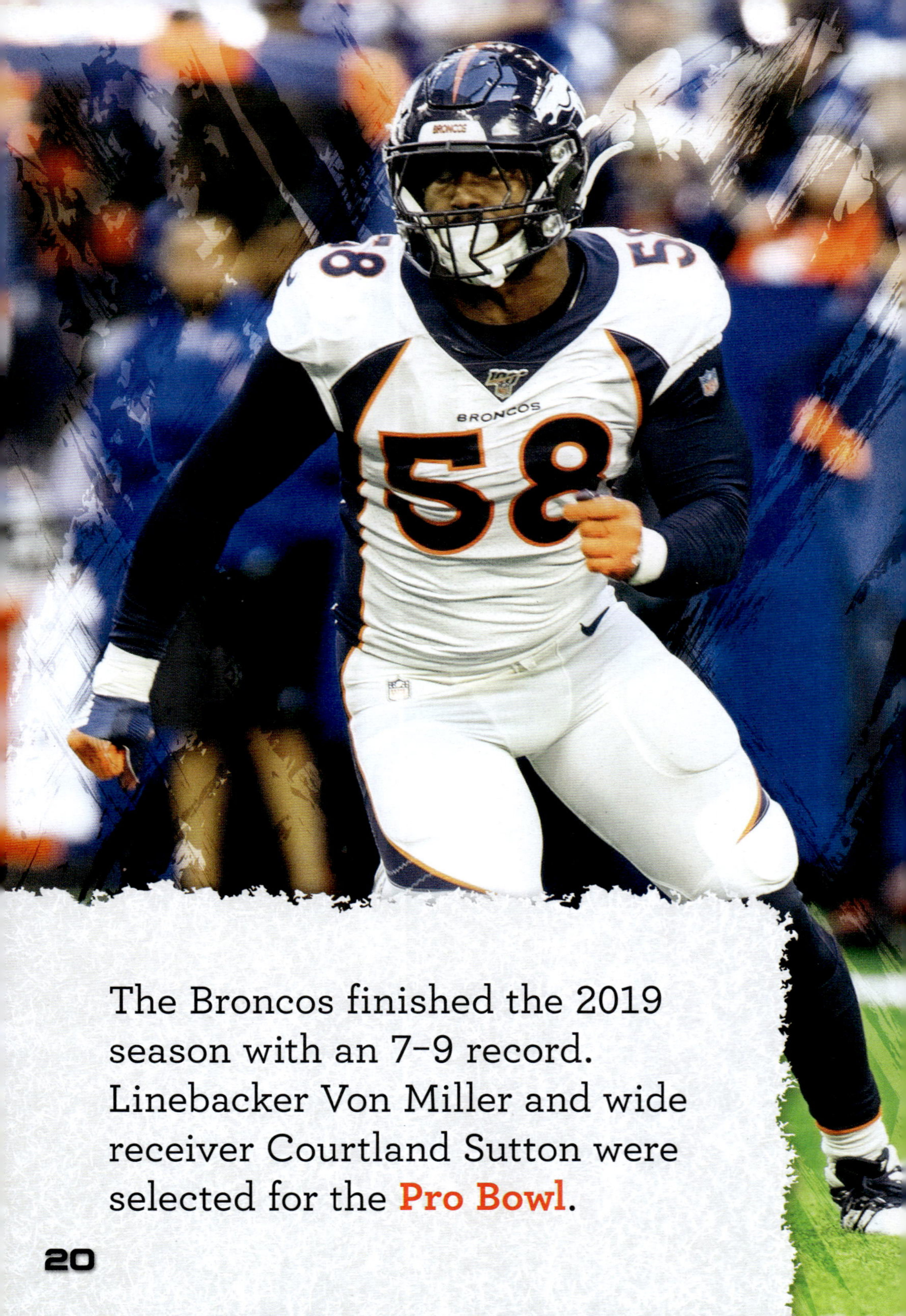

The Broncos finished the 2019 season with an 7-9 record. Linebacker Von Miller and wide receiver Courtland Sutton were selected for the **Pro Bowl**.

21

2020 came with some extra safety rules due to COVID-19. In week 12, **QB** Drew Lock had to quarantine. The rest of Denver's QBs were also in quarantine.

Wide receiver Kendall Hinton was pulled up from the **practice squad** to play starting QB in his first ever NFL game.

HALL OF FAME

Quarterback John Elway led the Broncos to five **Super Bowls** and two wins! He had 51,475 passing yards by the time he retired. That is more than any other Bronco! Elway was **inducted** into the Pro Football Hall of Fame in 2004.

Shannon Sharpe had more receptions, receiving yards, and receiving touchdowns than any other tight end in the NFL when he retired. He also went to two **Super Bowls** with the Broncos and won! Sharpe became a member of the Pro Football Hall of Fame in 2011.

BRONCOS
18
18
BRONCOS
18
Super Bowl 50
NFL
Wilson

During the 2013 season, Peyton Manning threw for 5,477 yards and 55 touchdowns with the Broncos, both NFL records! He led the Broncos to two **Super Bowls** during his four years with the team. Manning was **inducted** into the Pro Football Hall of Fame in 2021.

GLOSSARY

induct – to admit someone as a member of an organization.

practice squad – a specialty team of 16 players to practice with an NFL team but not play in actual games.

Pro Bowl – a game played once a year between two teams comprised of the NFL's all-stars.

quarterback (QB) – the player on the offensive team that directs teammates in their play.

Super Bowl – the NFL championship game, played once a year.

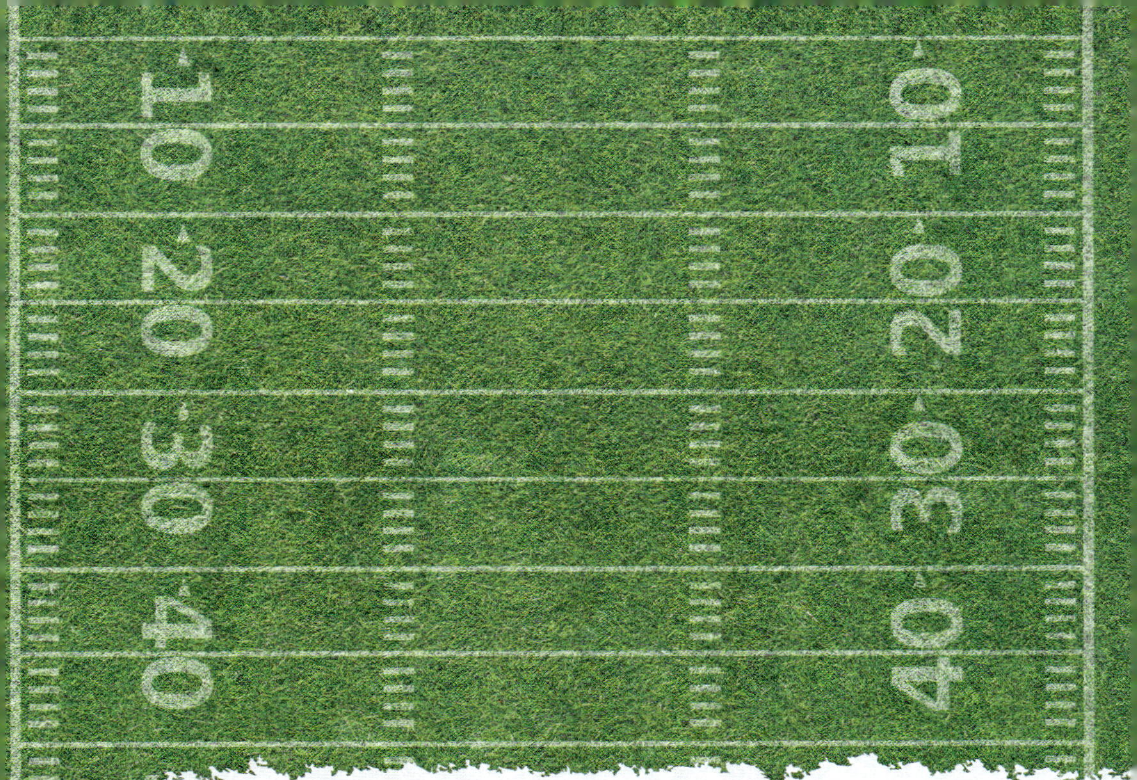

ONLINE RESOURCES

To learn more about the Denver Broncos, please visit abdobooklinks.com or scan this QR code. These links are routinely monitored and updated to provide the most current information available.

INDEX